I0558621

THOUGHTS ON
MARRIAGE

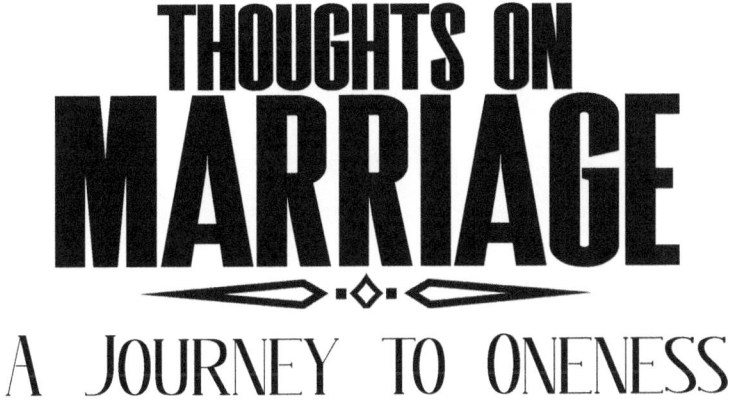

THOUGHTS ON MARRIAGE

A JOURNEY TO ONENESS

PAUL N. MUNDEN

ARPress
ILLUMINATING IDEAS,
EMPOWERING VOICES

Copyright © 2024 by Paul N. Munden

All rights reserved. No part of this publication may be reproduced, distributed, or transmitted in any form or by any means, including photocopying, recording, or other electronic or mechanical methods, without the prior written permission of the copyright owner and the publisher, except in the case of brief quotations embodied in critical reviews and certain other noncommercial uses permitted by copyright law. For permission requests, write to the publisher, addressed "Attention: Permissions Coordinator," at the address below.

ARPress
45 Dan Road Suite 5
Canton MA 02021
Hotline: 1(888) 821 0229
Fax: 1(508) 545 7580

Ordering Information:
Quantity sales. Special discounts are available on quantity purchases by corporations, associations, and others. For details, contact the publisher at the address above.

Printed in the United States of America.

ISBN 13: Paperback   979-8-89356-040-4
            eBook   979-8-89356-041-1

Library of Congress Control Number: 2024903094

CONTENTS

APPENDICES

COPYRIGHTS

Scripture taken from the NEW AMERICAN STANDARD BIBLE,
Copyright 1960, 1962, 1963, 1971, 1972, 1975, 1977, 1995 by The
Lockman Foundation. Used by permission. www.Lockman.org

You Want Me to Change?

I don't believe I can change
(I have a new career)

I can't change the way I think
(I have a new car)

I am what I am
(God says change your direction)

I'd like to change
(Can someone change, really change?)

We both should change
(His commandments are not burdensome)
 I John 5:3

Let's change!
(Submit to one another) Ephesians 4:25

Honey, I love you
(God said- It is not good for man to be alone)
Genesis 2:18

By: Paul N. Munden, 2016

INTRODUCTION

A very old memory returned to my thoughts. I knew the memory was very old as I was a child standing on a sofa that is remembered as both being well worn and particularly located in the house in which I was raised. One day, my mother passed by, exiting the kitchen to my left heading further back in the house to my right. She paused briefly, looked at and yet spoke through and beyond me. She stated, "there has to be more to marriage than this". I knew she was not expecting me to respond. She was not really speaking to me. And yet, I heard her dismay, her struggle. She moved on with her day, and so did I with child's play. So, the question of the "more to marriage" was implanted, and I became an observer and ponderer of marriage which was the best I could manage. As to my parents, from all that happened or at least what I remember, they spent their lives together finding both less and more in marriage. More did win out though less had a strong role at times.

For me then, the task of making marriage "more", and avoiding the "less" became a goal. Discovering the "more" was later added to teenager ambitions for adulthood. Do not all teens swear to themselves to not repeat their parent's past mistakes? Only to learn by the age of mid to late twenties that they are carrying their parents uncured burdens.

My goal here is to write about the "more". There are many marriage writings that seek to improve and increase the "more". The writers are better skilled at addressing the subject and associated specifics, much of which has to do with communications. Their efforts correct misunderstandings and mistakes, which is very helpful. (As I purposely avoided most of those writings over approximately the last

40 years to allow me to write my own thoughts, I am ignorant of their more recent efforts.)

In my choosing to write about marriage, I am concerned with discovering the "more" through answering another question along the lines of "How do you know you are succeeding in marriage?" How does one speak with confidence about us? Is it by having a good day, a good vacation, a good week together? These are all excellent stories. Any good time and experience is to be applauded.

My vantage point is described as follows. I would rate our marriage very high on the success scale. I would measure myself as still in pursuit of perfection, having not come near such a state. However, I would also consider that there have been moments or glimpses into what is both perfection and beyond humanity. So, I am purposely writing about a state of marriage to which I still pursue. So, I hope that the reader will find some language here to assist in creating words to describe a good marriage, to help any marriage move in a positive direction along the marriage scale ranking. I also hope that those whose marriages are already succeeding beyond the words I will write will find cause to rejoice in their marriage achievements. I hope their marriages continue to grow.

RELATIONAL FOUNDATION

Blessed Trinity
Where the Father, Son and Holy Spirit
Are one
Love me, made in God's image
Possessing mysteries of my own
Known only and fully to God

Blessed Trinity
Who saved me from death
Who gave me hope in life and a hope for life
In a body moving closer to decay
To a time of departure

Blessed Trinity
Appointing me for glory
That my departure will bring you praise
As I add my voice to the throng
Of grateful worshippers

Blessed Trinity
Who lives beyond time
Relating before time
one being in a relationship of three
Acting as one with one mind
Living the command given to man to love with heart, soul and mind
Blessed Trinity

By: Paul N. Munden, 2019

HYMN

Holy, Holy, Holy, Lord God Almighty
Text: Reginald Heber (1826)

Holy, holy, holy! Lord God Almighty!
Early in the morning our song shall rise to thee.
Holy, holy, holy! Merciful and mighty,
God in three persons, blessed Trinity!

Holy, holy, holy! All the saints adore thee,
casting down their golden crowns around the glassy sea;
cherubim and seraphim falling down before thee,
which wert, and art, and evermore shalt be.

Holy, holy, holy! Though the darkness hide thee,
though the eye of sinful man thy glory may not see,
only thou art holy; there is none beside thee,
perfect in power, in love and purity.

Holy, holy, holy! Lord God Almighty! All thy works shall praise thy
name, in earth and sky and sea.
Holy, holy, holy! Merciful and mighty,
God in three persons, blessed Trinity.

TRINITARIAN ONENESS

Holy, Holy, Holy begins the monumental hymn by Heber. God in three persons, blessed Trinity ends the hymn. God's Holiness and God's nature, two great revelations and mysteries are stated and applauded in the hymn. God created mankind in His image. He imparted to us our human reason and our human emotions. To those who learned singing from a hymnal, these words are familiar. Three Holy's are a sequence that compels humans to bow with angels before God in worship.

The living, triune God, inhabiting an unapproachable light[1] (The Lockman Foundation), speaks to our very approachable dark humanity. He exists in a form and nature different from ours, and resides in a place where He measures time different from us. [2]We live within time; He exists outside of time. In our understanding, His nature is distinguished as one of attributes without limit. His understanding is without limit; His love is without limit, etc. It is His nature as infinite and eternal with immeasurable limits that makes it impossible to describe Him fully, being limited by the language available to us.

---

[1] *(New American Standard Bible),* I Timothy 6:16
[2] II Tim. 3:8

When God made the earth, sun, moon, stars, etc., He also created the measurement of time which we measure by the motions of the heavenly bodies. We measure our age by the passage of time. As we age, we grow old. We are born at a point in time, and we die at a point in time. Tombstones memorialize these dates. During our short lives[3], we grow from infancy to adult. There is a stage of life when strength, health and understanding are increasing. Then, there is a stage of life when strength, health and understanding are decreasing. We call the time of increase, as "advancing towards maturity". We call the time of decrease "aging". In God's dwelling place, time does not pass. Rather, God observes our time from an existence outside of time.

God's existence as a Trinity, as three in one, as one expressed as three, does not easily reconcile with our ideas of deity. We have belief systems with no God, with one God, with many Gods. We have belief systems where there is no border between God and Man, where the physical is also the spiritual.

When we seek to understand and describe the Trinity, language reaches a limit. God's full existence is larger than the words available to us. Nonetheless, it is the trinitarian nature of God which provides us with much of importance, of which our imperfect words can speak truly. The design of marriage benefits from a trinitarian creator origin.

---

[3]"Yet you do not know what your life will be like tomorrow. You are *just* a vapor that appears for a little while and then vanishes away." James 4:14

First, the eternal Trinity, where the existence of the Father, Son, and Holy Spirit, as three in one, tells us that the one God has always existed in relationship. The three intra-communicate, intra-commune. Thus, this triune God has never been alone, as though He needed a friend. Further, the creatures made in His image can communicate with each other as He gave us that aspect of Himself. He has always made a way for His special creation to communicate with Him. He is the only independent and free being who can and did choose to create this world and all that is in it; a choice He made. Yet, no part of creation contains His essence. Were all of God's creation cease to exist, He would remain unchanged, suffering no damage or loss of essence. [4]Further, in choosing to create, He chose to create humans, male and female, after his image and likeness.[5] He made them to become one.[6] Because He is one, it is possible for us to become one. We do not become one as He is one, but rather one according to His creative design. That our natures are marred by our rebellion against God, certainly affects our realization of being one. But, His nature does not fall short of being one. He is always and perfectly one and three. In their unity, the three do not cease to exist as though run through a blender. Then, God is three. Yet, the three are not separated from each other. So, God is one and yet three; three and yet one.

Whether we are a male and female being one, and ascribing to further become one in marriage or whether we live singly with God as our sole affection[7], God welcomes and relates to our person. He is the first and final friend to our existence. By His design, we will still have a name of our own in His eternal home.

---

[4]Further, God does not involve himself, his own being, in the process. (of creation) Creation is not a part of him or an emanation from his reality. Erickson, pg. 397.
[5]Genesis 1:27
[6]Genesis 2:24
[7]I Corinthians 7:32

TRINATARIAN CREEDS

The ancient creeds provide weight to Christian doctrine. The Apostles Creed dates to the 4th Century. With an emphasis upon Jesus Christ, it reads as follows.

APOSTLES CREED

I believe in God, the Father, Almighty, maker of heaven and earth, and in Jesus Christ, his only Son, our Lord. who was conceived of the Holy Spirit, and born of the Virgin Mary, who suffered under Pontius Pilate, was crucified, died and was buried, descended into hell, rose again from the dead on the third day, ascended into heaven and is seated at the right hand of God the Father Almighty, who will come again to judge the living and the dead. I believe in the Holy Spirit, the holy catholic Church[8], the communion of saints, the forgiveness of sins, the resurrection of the body, and the life everlasting. Amen.[9]

Although the word Trinity does not appear in the Bible, there is much evidence of the nature of God as a Trinity in scripture. Here is one specific example. Jesus conversing with His Father—"And now, Father, glorify Me together with Yourself, with the glory which I had with You before the world was." John 17:5

---

[8] catholic meaning universal as used here.
[9] The Book of Common Prayer, pg.96

Jesus is requesting a renewal of a remembered shared glory; "glorify Me,. With *the* glory". Some bold disciples of Jesus once requested thrones to the left and right of Jesus.[10] They held significant dreams of glory. The Christian's soul swells with the hope of walking streets of gold in a city lit by the presence of God.[11] But, none of us speak like Jesus. When we speak of glory, we speak of what we hope to receive per the promises of God. It is a glory of our own according to our heavenly reward given to us by the Grace of God. In no way would we consider the glory God gives us even a small piece of His Glory. His Glory is beyond us, and extends from His very essence. Jesus is speaking of a shared Glory. He is speaking as the Son of God, as God Himself. Here, He is speaking as someone who has shared deity with the Father.

The Athanasian Creed is another ancient statement with a special focus upon the Trinitarian nature of God. Thought to have been written in the 4th Century, it is datable from approximately 500 AD.

ATHANASIAN CREED

Whosoever will be saved, before all things it is necessary that he hold the catholic faith. Which faith except everyone do keep whole and undefiled, without doubt he shall perish everlastingly. And the catholic faith is this: That we worship one God in Trinity, and Trinity in Unity, neither confounding the persons, nor dividing the substance.

For there is one Person of the Father, another of the Son, and another of the Holy Spirit. But the godhead of the Father, of the Son, and of the Holy Spirit, is all one, the glory equal, the majesty co-eternal.

Such as the Father is, such is the Son, and such is the Holy Spirit. The Father uncreated, the Son uncreated, and the Holy Spirit uncreated. The Father incomprehensible, the Son incomprehensible, and the Holy Spirit incomprehensible.

---

[10] Mark 10:35-40
[11] Revelation 21:23

The Father eternal, the Son eternal, and the Holy Spirit eternal. And yet they are not three eternals, but one Eternal.

As also there are not three incomprehensible, nor three uncreated, but one Uncreated, and one Incomprehensible. So likewise the Father is Almighty, the Son Almighty, and the Holy Spirit Almighty. And yet they are not three almighties, but one Almighty.

So the Father is God, the Son is God, and the Holy Spirit is God. And yet they are not three gods, but one God.

So likewise the Father is Lord, the Son Lord, and the Holy Spirit Lord. And yet not three lords, but one Lord.

For as we are compelled by the Christian verity to acknowledge each Person by Himself to be both God and Lord, so we are also forbidden by the catholic religion to say that there are three gods or three lords.

The Father is made of none, neither created, nor begotten. The Son is of the Father alone, not made, nor created, but begotten. The Holy Spirit is of the Father, neither made, nor created, nor begotten, but proceeding.

So there is one Father, not three fathers; one Son, not three sons; one Holy Spirit, not three holy spirits.

And in the Trinity none is before or after another; none is greater or less than another, but all three Persons are co-eternal together and co-equal. So that in all things, as is aforesaid, the Unity in Trinity and the Trinity in Unity is to be worshipped.

He therefore that will be saved must think thus of the Trinity.

Furthermore, it is necessary to everlasting salvation that he also believe rightly the Incarnation of our Lord Jesus Christ. For the right faith is, that we believe and confess, that our Lord Jesus Christ, the Son of God, is God and man; God, of the substance of the Father, begotten before the worlds; and man of the substance of his mother, born in the world; perfect God and perfect man, of a rational soul and human flesh subsisting.

Equal to the Father, as touching His godhead; and inferior to the Father, as touching His manhood; who, although He is God and man, yet he is not two, but one Christ; one, not by conversion of the godhead into flesh but by taking of the manhood into God; one altogether; not by confusion of substance, but by unity of person. For as the rational soul and flesh is one man, so God and man is one Christ; who suffered for our salvation, descended into hell, rose again the third day from the dead. He ascended into heaven, He sits at the right hand of the Father, God Almighty, from whence He will come to judge the quick and the dead. At His coming all men will rise again with their bodies and shall give account for their own works. And they that have done good shall go into life everlasting; and they that have done evil into everlasting fire.

This is the catholic faith, which except a man believe faithfully, he cannot be saved.[12]

This discussion has focused upon the nature of God. The importance of beginning a discussion of any aspect of God's creation and design, including marriage, with a discussion of God's nature cannot be overstated. The benefits of such a focus also cannot be overstated. As we meditate upon the infinite God, we step a little closer to His perspective upon His universe.

As to His design for our relationships, and particularly for marriage, noted are at least two aspects of God's nature as both relevant and discernible. As stated previously, that God is a Trinity means that communication already existed before Creation, and was then designed into humanity created in God's image. Humans communicate with each other because God already experiences communication within the Trinity.

A second aspect is that God exists as a unity in diversity. The three persons of the Godhead, while a unity, retain their distinctions.

---

[12] The Book of Common Prayer, pg. 864-865

TRINITARIAN MARRIAGE
MARITAL ONENESS

God's plan for marriage is inspired by Himself. Even as He created man and woman individually in His image,[13] so He created marriage in His image. We have the possibility to image God individually and as a married couple. He created the two to become one; to achieve oneness.

God made male and female. "Us" made man. God is one and yet an "Us". The Father, the Son and the Holy Spirit were unified in their decision to create a likeness of themselves. A limited likeness of an infinite God was bestowed upon man and woman. The one true God, existing in three persons fashioned each to be His, and these two to become one. "What God has joined together..."[14]. The two were purposed to image the oneness of God. Following a Trinitarian model, a third added to these two is primarily God. The Holy Trinity fashioned a Holy trinity. Further, as two become one, the union they share also becomes a third. A union not separate from themselves, as the persons of the Godhead are not separate from each other. (It seems that God has made room in creation for more thirds.)

In an effort to distinguish our earthly unions from God's perfect triune existence, the following utilizes a mix of apophatic [15]and cataphatic [16] statements. Consider the ideals of marriage vs the imperfections

---

[13]Genesis 1:26,27

[14]Matthew 19:6

[15]Apophatic – the use of negative theology to describe God. Example – our best love falls short of His immeasurable love.

[16]Cataphatic- the use of positive theology to know and describe God. Example-We serve a personal God who loves.

typical of marriages as you read this.

God is not in disagreement with Himself. Jesus never says the Father is not doing His job. The Holy Spirit never complains of not getting enough credit. The Holy Spirit never seeks to win followers to Himself alone. None of the three are jealous of the other's position or role. Yet, there is only one God. They are in unity. They are three in one. None claims to be smothered by the other. There is nothing of their unity, which would cause one to claim that being bound to the other is a burden. None would say their existence is less fulfilled than if they were free from the other. None has ever threatened to walk out on the other. None has ever sought a divorce. They are content in their unity. They are content in their diversity. God is so perfect that He may call Himself such without pride, without any exaggeration. He loves perfectly, and so may define love by Himself. God is love; the three is love. God was always this way. There was never a time when He did not love. There was never a time when the three did not love. There was never a time when that love changed. He is never more nor less loving, and thus eternal in fact.

Such words are always true for God. He always lives in a place where these words of love surround Him and are powerfully exercised by Him. God lives in unapproachable light[17]. But, His very approachable love for us causes Him to request us to come. And, He has made a way for us to do so. He was never alone. He purposed that men and women would never be alone. And, He promises that we may love each other as He intended. He purposes that couples still marry and become one and not be alone.

When your marriage exhibits oneness, the Trinitarian God is imaged upon earth. When you taste oneness together, the Trinitarian concept of God becomes plausible to your heart and mind. When you love each other in this way, then only death can part you. And, that was what you promised, wasn't it.

---

[17] I Timothy 6:16

Whether we are a male and female being one and becoming one in marriage or whether we live singly with God as our sole affection, God welcomes and relates to us. He is the first and final friend to our existence. By His design, we will still have a name of our own in His eternal presence. Meanwhile, we have the opportunity and potential blessing of marriage, where we learn about oneness here first before we set aside the oneness of marriage in joining the final oneness beyond all marriage oneness. We will see God for who He is. We will see each other as He really sees us.

Another way to describe a path to marital oneness might be to travel a road that reduces the distance between what my dear wife will finally become in God's presence, and the current perception of who she is.

THIRDS

Observing a Trinitarian model of relationship leads one to ask of marriage, "Where is the third?" A marriage of two creates a union, a oneness. To this union of two might be added a third. The first and best third is God. Genesis describes an open communication between Adam and Eve and God. There are three here. Any marriage would do well to follow this model with God as an important third to the pair. This chapter addresses the idea that there are, in both design and practice, other thirds to attach to our couple.

Children add a "third" quality. As a couple image themselves in another, the mystery of what marital oneness births is held in their arms and nurtured. As humanity and creation are "fruitful and multiply", a multitude of images walking with God in the "cool of the day"[18] would by their incalculable number and variety more simply be called infinite. The image of God is imaged by His works, including His sons and daughters. As His daughters and sons marry and become one, their marriage images Gods' nature in a way they do not separately.

So, children are special thirds that find our married pair modeling the miracle of the creation of humanity. If mankind had not separated themselves from God through severe disobedience, then the original pair would still live and walk and communicate. To that original pair would be added all the pairs since. The total of these thirds would by now be immeasurable. They might be described as a practical infinity. An infinite God creating a finite pair that procreated to a practical infinity. (See how death damages the image of God in the eyes of man.)

---

[18] Genesis 3:8

There are other thirds in our world, even in our world that is estranged from God. All of these thirds, beginning with children, are loved by their parents. Children bring joy to their parents. And, they are, while their parents live, of ever concern to their parents. Parents never stop parenting. It just takes different forms as parents and children age. While the love of our pairs for their children cannot match the love of God, they love as best they can, and receive, in turn the love these thirds, these children, can requite.

OTHER THIRDS

For others, thirds take the form of what we refer to as pets. Pets offer far less than children made in the image of God. Nonetheless, they are important companions to their masters. With far less time to live, their masters must grieve their loss. (I think it a less than full life for couples who might parent children, to substitute a pet as a third from whom to give and receive affection.) Still, the design of the created world makes room to love and be loved by pets. Pets make great stories. Consider the following essay.

MAN'S BEST FRIEND?-date 2002

"Leading a dog's life" would not mean the same thing in every country in the world. But, in my neighborhood a dog who never loses a drop of sweat in a household chore without ridicule, who is able to make time demands of others 24/7, whose living quarters are better than many, and who eats well besides is "leading a dog's life". We should all live so well.

I do not remember when our dog became a full-fledged member of the family. When he arrived he was a dog. And, then he was given a name. And then, we began to learn his ways and he ours. Being a rather stubborn animal, he was more intent upon us learning his ways and less interested in learning ours. Eventually, the differences were resolved, and his "probation" period ended. Having graduated to "dog for life" status, he became eligible to become human. Upon his death, he will be lionized and beautified, something closer to what this Pekingese already thinks of himself.

Another example--I received an advertisement in the mail suggesting that I should have my dogs teeth brushed professionally. Being somewhere between an old timer in my views on dog care and just plain ignorant, I was amazed that such a procedure was even offered, much less utilized. But, what struck me most was the photograph in the flyer. Centered in the picture was this gorgeous golden haired Labrador Retriever fresh from a beauty session, with a coat to die for. To the left and right were a smiling veterinarian and a smiling owner. The animal was positioned for the photograph in a manner that made the dog look human. The dog was clearly a dog. But, the picture was clearly a portrait, and the look of the picture so much like a family photo that I had to sit and stare at the picture just to take it in. Dog's head was placed at even eye level as the human heads to the left and right, and a little out front of each. It was a definite, "Look mom, no cavities" type picture. If I had been present at the photography session, I would have expected the dog to leave on two legs, not four. Seeing the animal step down to all fours would have been disappointing. The language and appearance of the flyer matched the photograph.

The day a pet, any pet, enters a home is a day of celebration. Everyone wants to see it, watch what it does, how it eats, how it moves. Bedtime for the children is an especially delayed event. They have to see it one more time before sleep. They want to see and know that it is safe, etc. There are high expectations placed upon the creature. Even higher expectations are placed upon how the creature will add to the family life and the life of the owner. Should the creature die prematurely, as some certainly do, the loss may be such that another like it is not acquired. Let's try something else.

There is not much expected from a jar of fireflies. Frogs normally do not survive the tastes of parents, and are let go. Turtles rise a little higher. Fish readily come and go unless they live a long time. Then, their passing is noted. I've never heard much discussion about pigs, lizards, alligators, etc. I grew up with a friend who had a pet chicken. We all received dyed chicks in those days on Easter. They died so quickly that their passing was barely noted. My friend had one who grew to be an adult. The chicken ran about like chickens do with feathers still tinted orange from whatever color it was to begin with. When it was hit by a car, it lost the use of one leg. So, the one legged chicken hopped about. I've no remembrance of how it passed.

I've little knowledge of horses. But, it seems to me that a horse might begin as a pet. Eventually, they all seem to be horses. I think that is because they cost more to own and need more care than children. If I had been groomed as a horse in my formative years, I would probably be the president by now. Then there are the "higher" forms of pet life, namely cats and dogs.

THERE IS GREAT HOPE IN ACQUIRING A DOG.- dated 2002

There is great hope in acquiring a dog. Children and adults alike are captivated by a puppy; even better a litter of them rolling about. Bringing one home and watching the relationship with the family develop makes good conversation amongst family and friends. Whether the creature be purebred and trained or a mutt of unknown and suspect origin, the hope of a long and mutually enjoyable relationship is a common and widely held belief.

A rare story tells of the really bad dog. The really just plain horrible dog is typically ascribed to failed breeding and/or poor treatment. Even then the animal is not at fault. And, regardless of the failure, there is someone who will take the animal and give it *another* try. One person's disgust is another's challenge and joy. And, so stories are told and retold of the reformed and now lovely creature. The result of such victories supports the accurate view that your dog's relationship with you is what you work to see it become. Neglect and cruelty make a monster. Love and discipline make a life-long friend.

Marriage is not accompanied by the optimism of eventual success no matter the history. Couples marry with the hope of success. But, even a poll of those in attendance at the wedding ceremony will not support such optimism. The astounding failure of marriage to result in what marriage purports to promise or even to result in what each spouse promises to the other places the expectation of success at something less than that of acquiring a dog.

But, then dogs really have the better of it. People who acquire a dog expect to spend time developing the relationship after acquiring it. They may attend obedience classes together. They openly discuss and inquire of others how to succeed. They read various manuals.

They regularly consult with their vets. When the animals act poorly, they easily forgive the creature. (As we will see further, marriage is frequently left to survive with as much neglect as possible.)

Having "a dog's life" is desirable. The manner in which they should be cared for is well-documented. And, there is general agreement between professionals on how a dog should be raised and managed. Dogs are pampered, groomed, and well-fed. They are guarded from dangers. Their breeding is carefully controlled. Cruelty against them is really scorned upon, and socially unacceptable. Letting them roam free and breed wherever and whenever is unacceptable. Leashes are acceptable. Their offspring is cuddled and carefully passed to worthy families.

To repeat, there is great hope in acquiring a dog.

The bride says I do
The groom says I don't
The fights go on til
The marriage says I won't

(This all sounds like insecurity to me;
no love, no strength of promise I see.)

When my wife and I hold one another,
We know for sure there is no other.
No doubts or fears are in our brains
Our smiles are real, our pleasure unstained

How, you say, did we find this?

My wife and I vowed
Before God and man
That we belonged to each other
From then until death

Jesus strengthens this promise
In our hearts and minds
We're determined to keep it
In joy throughout our lives

You must see!

Love is much more than a
Feeling or rise
It's much, much more than the smiles in our eyes
For love is the will, the decision of mind
It says – "I will not quit!"
"I've promised to be thine!"

Paul Munden
1982

COURTSHIP LOVE

Courtship is not a word in much daily use. In some sections of our society it is still used to describe a process of preparation for a formal covenant of marriage, a process used in lieu of dating. As a formal process, rules of courtship are put into place to help manage the development of the pre-marital relationship as well as better define the understanding of married life as two journey on a trajectory towards marriage. However, courtship as used here will be defined more broadly.

The actual types of relationships in which two might participate vary considerably. From an afternoon walk in the sunshine to a weekend get-away to living together for a period of years, there are many descriptions in use. Marriage is defined here as a relationship with covenants formalized by the participants. Where you are present in a marriage ceremony that includes vows, which are promises, you are hearing covenant statements. Marriage formalization need not be in a culturally understood setting, i.e. a marriage ceremony with vows. Two who have long lived together, living out covenant commitments are here considered married, official ceremony or not. Courtship is defined here as any relationship which intentionally lacks some or all of the types of covenant commitments two people make with each other. Thus, Courtship is defined as any relationship other than marriage. Two who have long lived together, but still maintain some significant measure of individual reserve are not here married. Since, by their agreed upon lack of covenant(s), they are intending something other than marriage, the two are still keeping courtship aspects within their relationship. These relationships along with all others of temporary duration are outside of our definition of marriage.

A marriage is a relationship whereby two, one male and one female, purpose to become one. A marriage may begin with limited purposes and limited covenants. But, over time, more covenants will be added. Where they find need for an additional covenant, and refuse to add it to their relationship, they may even drift apart and separate. No matter how vague the relationship begins, covenants must be added and possibly formalized for oneness to occur. Covenants are necessary to marriage, and their best beginning is a formalization. Meanwhile, courtship relationships are those where one or both parties select a portion of their life which they live for themselves. Or, to say it differently, there are areas of their life that they choose to live alone rather than together.

Our primary concern here is with two trajectories of courtship, and involves two single people who are capable of entering into a covenant of marriage. One trajectory will lead to marriage. The others will not. One is labeled as a path to oneness. The other is a path to aloneness.

COURTSHIP AS A PATH TO ONENESS

People meet everywhere. "How did you meet?" is a common party icebreaker. Dating services facilitate meetings. Gatherings from schools to clubs to concerts to churches are door openers. If we take the time to observe others during any of these gatherings, the mystery of attraction is soon on display. Many relationships remain no more than acquaintances or alternately, friendships. There was clearly little potential for growth beyond friendship to one or both. Both return to being general members of society available for the next mystery of attraction to happen. And, this time, it looks "serious" to all. Talking to you is very important. Talking to others is unimportant. Seeing you again is worth the time and travel; seeing others not so much. Even now, there is and will remain significant opportunities for failure. The ever present trend towards selfishness can become intolerable resulting in the end of the relationship. Destructive selfishness can be intensely present in one or more key areas of life. Sometimes, it is an accumulation found present in most every area of life, a selfish person. At any rate, the relationship ends finding each party again alone. They will chose to not marry. Each will be sad for a time and be alone in that sadness. How did all this potential fail so badly?

In attending a 1997 family preservation event in Washington DC, our group of men took an early morning subway to RFK stadium. Looking about on that ride, I noticed a young woman sitting near me who did not appear to want to be there. She was not looking at other people. She was shifting uneasily in her seat, nursing a blanket, shedding tears, and struggling to hold more back. Our group soon exited the subway, but I never forgot this poor young woman for whom an out of place grief was unavoidably openly on display. It could have been caused by many events, but had the appearance of the type of rejection associated with a breakup or at least significant relationship disappointment.

WHOS AND WHATS

Courtship is the beginning of a lifelong journey to be a *who* and not a *what*. In speaking of a human performing a humanizing act, *who or Whom* is used. In speaking of someone performing a dehumanizing act, *what* takes the place of *who*. In courtship, presenting *whos* to our intended love is a must. Too many *whats* end a relationship.

A classic struggle for a what to become a who is seen in the Frankenstein movies with Boris Karloff. Pieced together with others parts, this living creature is struggling to be human, to be a who. But, his evil deeds reinforce his monster status as a what which better describes a creature doing what he does. Being a what is unfavorable. And, so the creature is tormented internally as he struggles to become a who and hounded by enemies determined to destroy it, whatever it is.

In a last desperate plan, having a "mate" like other people is the creatures plan to become a who. In a famous scene where he meets his mate, he is rejected again as a horrible what. When that reaction reaches his soul, he despairs of life. He has failed to become a who, and being condemned to be a what he grant's everyone's wish and brings down the castle upon himself and his would be mate.

So, with our past and present, we endanger our relationships with deeds that make us whats. A child abused might become an adult abuser. An abuser is a what, and not a who. Tears and promises to change may be sincere, but a permanent change needs a miracle. As will be observable often in this book, Jesus Christ performs such miracles. He turns whats into whos.

A perfect date is marred by an angry tirade against a waitress, and then the manager. "What happened?" "What are you doing?"(Acting like a what.)

There are many who deeds as well. Flowers and courtesies help. Sincere words and intentions help. "I love you" with all its meaning helps. And, so our who works to show who qualities. Many would be what deeds are hidden, and some really do go away entirely as who expressions become who habits.

With a general mutual celebration of love, our couple becomes engaged and marry. Over time, both who and what qualities are expressed. The struggle to realize the promise of oneness may take years or may never happen as the whats win. Like the monster, hopes to become a who are destroyed.

COURTSHIP AS A PATH TO ONENESS, DATING SERIOUSLY

Ready or not you just met or saw a most interesting person. You have no real words to describe the feelings that passed through you. There were some of the usual that you associate with being in the presence of an attractive person. But there was something else, something with no name. It is that something accompanied by an inexplicable awkwardness. It's an embarrassment that I would endure if I could see you again.

From that moment, there could be days or even years before we are in the same room together again. Even at this stage of a relationship each couple begins to have their own story. They don't know when it started. But, they remember later that it did. A foreshadowing of the possibility of oneness. When next we meet, we start where we left off. Not like acquaintances who have to be reintroduced each time.

FOREVER WORDS

Strangely, at least I found it strange for me, was the use of phases like, "I will love you forever." "I love you" was enough, and likely all that was really heard. But, for some reason the relationship was causing me to embellish phrases of affection with what I call "forever words". I remember putting on paper, if you can believe it a phrase to the effect, "I see no end to you and I until we reach the sky". A poetic way of saying "to death do us part". Seems like these forever words and others like them are attempts to capture the measureless portions of the emotions that were presenting themselves for me to find some way to express.

Being measureless, they point to the existence of the infinite, of the infinite God who made the forever words possible. Thus, they function indirectly as evidence of the personal infinite God.

COURTSHIP HARMONY

During courtship, the focus of both parties is to discover what each holds in common. Every successful date results in an agreed upon temporary separation. For who would not want to spend every day, every moment with someone who is so loved and who so loves. The scales of fate tip increasingly heavy towards eternal bliss. Discovered differences are proclaimed to one and all as examples of why each *needs* the other or how they will complement. The strength of their mutual love and affection is considered by both to be all the stronger because their differences are so easily overcome. They are judging the future by the present. They are claiming to be in harmony, an acknowledged diversity in the midst of unity. The couple achieves courtship harmony.

To emphasize the importance of the desire for agreement, consider couples that "break up" before they marry. From the blind date to the serious almost married twosome, the bottom line explanation for an agreed end to the relationship will often include a statement to the effect that we "really had very little in common." Once that statement is made, all who hear will agree—It is time to move on. "Wow, it really is over between you two?" "Yes, you see, I realized we had very little in common." "But, you seemed so happy and got along so well." "I know, but the more I got to know him, the less we had in common."

MARRIAGE INCLUDING COVENANTS

On your wedding day, you celebrate all that has brought you to this act of commitment in the presence of witnesses. On the basis of your experience and the nature of how you define the marriage contract, you make promises, vows, covenants with each other. In spite of the possible forms of vows, few couples marry with the intention that the marriage will end in 2 years or 10 years. Both are love struck and certain that their love has "til death do us part" certainties.

As soon as possible after the wedding, you notice "new" differences between the two of you. Soon there will be more "new" differences. You will also change how you feel about some of the old differences. The revelation of these differences quickly moves to the frustration point. It is as though one partner is going out of their way to be different.

Really, these differences are manifesting themselves in the absence of the unified courtship focus of discovering unity. The couples are not trying to be different. They are no longer trying to only learn and discover what they have in common. As a result, there is more room for differences to show themselves. And, they do, don't they?

This reassertion of diversity virtually destroys the now mutually recognized limited harmony they achieved during courtship. The question, every couple must ask of themselves, and the effort of the successful marriage will be to journey to the more complex marital harmony. Can they achieve marital harmony?

EXPRESSIONS OF ETERNITY

Til death do us part---Mystically, the two become one immediately in the sexual act. Mystically and practically, it takes years to become one in other ways. In a growing marriage, the areas in which you are not one diminish over time. You will not mark the calendar the day you became one about X. You will simply notice over time that the total number of understandings between you have increased. And, the total number of matters where significant discussion is required decrease. Eliminating the debates indicates understandings. At some point in the relationship, you literally obtain glimpses of eternity. As your love for each other deepens, and the time of your marriage increases, you begin to forget what it was like to be single. You begin to forget what is was like to still have pockets of insecurity with each other. And, you begin to sense that your love for each other is becoming immeasurable. The taste of immeasurability is a taste of eternity. Your love for each other is such that it almost seems tangible. It is not a love which is without passion. Nor is it a love expressed in passion alone. The greatest hours of passion are models and examples of a love you experience for each other at moments when you are not even in each other's company or at times when passion is not an element at all. This is a taste of eternity. And, it is then a glimpse of the love of God, a glimpse of the love within the Trinity. Thus, you taste a moment of what God intends for marriage, even in a fallen world.

COURTSHIP MARRIAGE

As mentioned earlier, some, perhaps many enter into an arrangement that has some qualities of a covenant marriage, and lacks others. Quite a few relationships seem to include living together with a rather indetermined definition of the future. Each one has a different answer as to what the relationship is, and also what it will be. There is often an intention on the part of both to eventually marry. A common quality of such relationships is a measure of observable inequality between them. One may have the greater income. One may stay home with children. Both may have particular activities that they maintain as though single. Where they are equal is in the inability of one to make significant demands of the other. Not being married without any real vows, promises or covenants to bind them to each other, each is free to determine the limits of the requirements of affection.

COURTSHIP LOVE

There remain two myths of courtship that need explanation. Both are related as almost cause and effect. First, contrary to the emphasis upon the discovery of mutuality's, courtship love is really a time of maximizing good impressions, and also maximizing deceptions. As we generally see each other as mutually agreed, we are able to present our bests of everything. And, we are able to hide the worsts of everything. Thus, we are each working with incomplete pictures carefully crafted for our times together. We may even employ others for recommendations. Families may contribute to these pictures as they vacate gathering rooms to permit the lovers to live out their privacies with each other. Oh, it is still quite probable that we may explain our lives as we never have to anyone else. But, telling stories of our lives comes nowhere near putting the impact of such stories on display in the marriage.

The second myth, linked to the first, is that courtship dating is the most romantic time of our lives. It is quite common to hear one member of the later marriage reminisce back to the pre-marital relationship as the idyllic time in life with the other. When I hear such stories, I am greatly concerned for that marriage. One or both is not seeing clearly. And considering what was just said about the artificial elements of dating, neither may have ever seen clearly. A deepening and loving marriage should leave all the period of courtship behind in affections expressed, a fond memory and a good beginning to the later wealth of a happy marriage.

We married in the warmest church
On the brightest spring June day
We honey mooned near mountain streams
Sipping love we'd share always

We laughed through all the early years
Til the small ones came along
But sleepless nights and diapers changed
Some laughter into yawns

And then demands so pressing
Came up and sneaked inside
We laughed some still but argued
Big decisions to decide

Now, we still have a good laugh
It makes the nerves tense less
Stead of sipping love, we gulp our half
Seldom remember tenderness

It seems that life has stolen
What we once dreamed life would be
How'd it all become a jungle
Through which we hardly see?

And why did we quit laughing
We both wished the samest things
Did we change that much? So much?
We should have married in the winter not the spring

By: Paul N. Munden, 1982

DEMI-LOVE

Although the larger goal of this writing is to provide some positive vision for marriage, it is necessary to address how love falls short, how love fails. Loves failure is the theme of the next two chapters. In this chapter, love fails as a minimal effort of love is offered. Having been together for a time, it may be learned that a certain marital peace can be maintained through offering to the other actions we know will please them. Now, pleasing the other is preferred over choosing actions that displease. Most do not wish to live in a constant state of tension.

Demi-love occurs as the part of me that seeks to satisfy the self, conflicts with the part of me in relationship with another. To illustrate, consider the familiar argument that goes something like this. "You don't love me anymore!" Typically stated by a spouse, this is really a conclusive statement summarizing both the current discussion, and perhaps a number of others. The husband may respond with a, "Yes, I do love you," followed by a more lengthy list of proofs in the form of actions and accomplishments now driven by love for the other. This list might include but not limited to such items as basic faithfulness, more than adequate provision, fathering, all of which might be very true. And, the spouse is forced to admit that much, if not all of what he said, is true. So "why are you complaining?" Thus, the debate subsides to the satisfaction of neither. She knows she failed to make her point, her increasingly desperate point; he knows he does not understand her. Somewhere along his very adequate efforts at faithfulness, provision and fathering the basic promise in the marriage vow of giving priority to loving his wife was lost. He certainly loves, meaning all of the things he might say, but she is rarely, if ever now, his priority. Even the things they still do together have a feel to the spouse that she could be anybody, and the event would still, for him, be a success.

In the most extreme examples, this anybody becomes somebody else. In those marriages that return from that brink of disaster, something changes. But, what was going on in the first place?

I think the old debate is better argued by restating the accusation. It is not, "you don't love me anymore". Rather, it should go something like-"Loving me is no longer important to you". With a statement like this, all of the other provisions are acknowledged. However, the central failure is that his spouse has been demoted in priority. It is not that she is unloved. Rather, that he sets aside no time to love her. (Our couple may have an active sex life, and yet the emotional bond be quite tenuous.)

In this respect, he has not kept the vow to love her, to prefer her above all else. Loving everything around her, from which he also benefits, is not the same as loving her first and then loving all else. Thus, he has become self-deceived in believing that loving what he cares for is enough and a correct form of love for the two of them.

Behind this mask may reside other unspoken truths.

1. He is committed to a number of things in his life. Her status as the first priority has fallen beneath some of his other pursuits. Debates about where she ranks actually result in her moving to a lower rank. (Debate is time consuming, unpleasant, something for which neither has the time in their busy lives.) Finally, he may want another woman who "understands" his priorities and will accept a lower entry rank without complaint. Thus, he acquires what he wants from a woman without changing his personal priority queue. Or, to say it differently, he finds someone for which a demi-love life is totally okay. (Admittedly, there are many for whom even a demi-love existence would be an improvement over their zero or negative love experiences to date.)

2. To serve his priorities, including the roles his spouse manages, he offers as little love input as possible to in turn reap the most benefit and types of attention centered upon his happiness.

Those half-love or demi-hearted, demi-love expressions are known as such by his wife. She resents her diminished status. He is content with the arrangement, seeing a positive, even smug cost-benefit structure to their relationship.

3. The Christian view of humanity is that life experience is negatively distorted until Jesus Christ takes His proper place, and begins His unique humanizing work. In a marriage without a sufficient work of Christ, one or both of our marriage partners tend to seek from each other answers and changes that only God can provide. This error in sourcing is also a problem in marriages where both are Christians. (Typically, the work of Christ occurs unevenly over a lifetime.) So, part of her angst may truly be a need for a work of God in her life rather than a problem for her husband. He, of course, has the same need, and is often the harder heart of the two. It is quite common to find a Christian wife living with and praying for her unbelieving husband.

4. He may double down on the demi-love by increasing the amount of faint praise he offers. His own solution to the debate may be to offer an extra dose of more of the same demi-love.

SUMMARY

Demi-love is a distortion of love expressions. All such distortions possess the quality of personal reserve, of offering something less than the whole. They are exercises in preserving control, whereby the self is being loved along with a portion of love offered to the other. Demi-love does not build marital oneness. Rather demi-love contributes further to living life alone while sharing the same house. One and/or both of our marriage partners has made a life pattern of offering to the other words and attentions that are largely self-focused and fall way short of the lofty words of love promised to each other.

UNIMPORTANT LOVE

In the previous chapter, we looked briefly at how love is distorted in a manner that it is offered with less than a whole heart. This form of failure has been named Demi-love.

Another large category of loves' failure occurs when love, itself, is set aside entirely, where it is traded for something else. Thus, in both failures, love for the self is preserved. However, in demi-love, there is self-deception as the love for the self is masked by claims to love the other. Where love becomes unimportant, both love received and love given are significantly reduced. They are both filtered out of the marital life. (The failure to give is offset by a difficulty, even a justification of the lack of receipt.)

It takes time and heart to love. If life is devoted to increasing efficiencies or takes a utilitarian track, then the heart becomes less necessary. Stopping this life train at little towns along the way to love is a waste of time and energy. The coast to coast route, blown along by a cold unfeeling wind, arrives on time.

THE LIMITATION OF WEALTH IN ACQUIRING LOVE

Money can't buy me love- The Beatles

Many waters cannot quench love,
  neither can floods drown it.
If a man offered for love
  all the wealth of his house,
  he (or it) would be utterly despised.[19]

---

[19] Song of Solomon 8:7

The Beatles, the most seminal, creative band of my youth, produced a lyric that looked beyond the massive wealth pouring into their coffers to the fact that their wealth would not acquire adequate and true affection. Whether they knew it or not, they were restating a similar long known and discussed theme of a noted limitation of wealth.

In the biblical reference, which forms but a part of an older and larger discussion of marital, even erotic love, the unquenchable passion of love is acknowledged. And, in contrast, even King Solomon, with his vast wealth, would find both himself and his great wealth despised when offered to acquire adequate and true affection.

Where love becomes unimportant, a couple takes the great love that they share, including the potential of loving further, and begins to whittle it away.

They may even conspire to this whittling by agreement to unnecessary postponements of daily affection. And, there are certainly jobs and professions that place a heavy demand upon time and energy. None of these demands necessitate a casting aside of love.

But, then, there are those who take the postponements, deferrals and delays, and make a choice to give them permanence. They define an adequate love as one where no catch up on time lost is required, where the sacrifice of each of them loses significance. Then, even as the schedule of life changes, and more time becomes available, the coldness of a life lacking affection is now preferred. Love has a particular cost, a desired fulfillment that cannot be quenched. However, its kindling can be controlled and managed out of one's day so that drifting towards a life lived more alone than shared becomes a desirable pattern.

It's a hard world we live in
Being kicked is not enough
We're scratched, battered, hurt
You just have to be tough.

Hide your hurt, hide it good,
Walk proud, let no one know
Seek love while you can
You're passions are your goal

But real happiness, hard to find
Inside my heart still cries
My pains are so real
The pains, the pains inside

I'm stuck with this mixture
Of peace seeking and anger
My emotions an interlude
To forget my real hunger

Where is hope, is it there?
I've tried to find peace
I've given up my search
My pain will never cease

By: Paul N. Munden, 1982

Twoness, Oneness, Aloneness

Now, we are married. We are one in some ways, still two in others. Twoness is when I live like we're not married. I have my life and you have yours. I make the best choices for me. I do consider you as I make these choices. You need to accept these as my choices. It takes time to become one. While we are becoming one, we are still two. Twoness is not oneness. I am accustomed to twoness. It's what we shared when we were planning to become one. But, twoness only worked well when we were not so physically near each other all the time. When we only let each other see what we wished, then we were happy as two; now we are becoming one. You are seeing the other half of me. And, I am seeing the other half of you. With the previous hidden half now visible, we each see the whole of the other. In some, maybe many ways, seeing the whole is less appealing than seeing the half. It was more fun when two halves made a whole. But now, we are taking two wholes and trying to make them one as we promised. It was easier when you saw the half of me I wished to show you. And I liked you, sometimes better, when you only showed me the half you wanted me to see. But if our two is really to become one, we must see the whole of each other. And I must admit sometimes, even hope, that the whole of you is actually more interesting.

Now, I have decided that the oneness we have shared was poisoned by too much twoness. You wanted me to be one with you when you were not too busy being two. I wanted you to treat me like you were happy with the whole that was me, not just happy with the half of me you wished to be at one with.

Now I am alone. We were two and then one. We drifted apart, then purposed to move apart, to return to two. We showed each other the sweet, and now we offer each other the bitter. I struggled to keep my share of your sweet. You took it from me; replaced it with bitter. You are still trying to hurt me. Sometimes I feel we could try again to be one. But when I remember how we always ended up like we were two, then I choose to be alone. I don't want to be alone. But, I would rather be alone than be the two that were unable to become one. I live a lonely alone.

MAID? OR MAID?

Pondering the question of wifey
I am forced to conjutate
whether wifey is a maid?
or a maid?

The fairest maid I ever knew
espied from afar
my heart sinking, my eyes falling
searching the ground for an obelisk of hope
to renew my espying from afar
of the fairest maid I ever saw

At last, the unplanned day
of formal introduction
only three feet away and speaking to me!?
Should I hide behind my friends
or pray our meeting never ends
how foolish to expect to stand there forever
with the maiden

Several years beyond the wedding day
my maid is oft a maid
for children must be nourished
and dinners must be made

Tis better to remember my maid is still a maiden
one I still pursue as if
I was a gent-in-waiting

The taste of love each day divine
(I wrap each kiss in a stay fresh package)
For if wifey can love as a maid
I will love her as my maiden

By: Paul N. Munden 1985

INTRODUCTION TO "18TH ANNIVERSARY SCRIBBLE"

In giving thought to marriage, I have searched for anything I could find from past writings and notes. This spontaneous expression, written in 1994, was located on an old computer disk. Beth and I agreed to share this with you. Special expressions of love take many forms. They may be planned or spontaneous; may be gifts, crafts or other creative expressions. We selected this as it seems to have captured, for a moment, a glimpse of God's great image for our marriage. I am guessing that a request was made to share something in the church service. I probably started writing and time ran out to read it. Must have typed it up later.(see original note at bottom) Now, I am humbled in reading it. Beth appreciated it again; asked me where I found it?

18th Anniversary scribble

Our marriage has been a dance whose steps are too complex to completely relate. A days time is not sufficient for celebration.So we choose to celebrate it daily. Amidst our failures or interruption of that celebration, our loving and faithful God remains the most constant partner. In our marriage balance, there is a weight of joy far exceeding our capacity of utterable words. We are bonded together in a manner which permits liberty and protects privacy. Outside of our own intimacies, our children provide our most perpetual joys. We would further chronicle the details of God's faithfulness which eclipse and augment the details of our relationship but time does not permit. For our part, we will vacation shortly on a quest to find Utopia. Most fortunately, we will take some with us. Rejoice with us this day on our 18th anniversary.

Written during church on or near our 18th anniversary in 1994 in a mad scribble on the back of the church bulletin which Beth kept for some equally mad reason.

ONENESS

Eccl. 3:11 "He has also set eternity in their heart, yet so that man will not find out the work which God has done from the beginning even to the end."

In embarking upon a description of oneness, a description of the type of union a man and woman both aim for and yet fail to fully realize, the initial Bible verse above is informative. God has made man in His image. Included in that image is a desire to experience eternity. And yet, that inspiration to pursue and nature of desire for eternity are disclosed to be impossible to accomplish. Man will be limited to what God discloses even as he will desire for more than God has revealed. God has revealed more than enough for our marriages to thrive. Thus, a significant amount of marital oneness is achievable, even in this world of sin, this world of disobedience and marriage failure.

PREPARATION

The best beginning really starts while single, with valuing a spoken word. Do either our man or woman, preparing to marry, have a habit of disregarding their own words? Are their promises worthless? Can a lie serve a holy purpose? If this pattern of devaluing words is true of their lives before marriage, then their spoken formalized vows in the presence of God and witnesses will not carry the weight of obligation that they should. However, if we are speaking of a man and woman, both of whom have stood by their own words in matters outside of marriage, then their spoken formalized marital vows will carry real meaning. (If you live by your words in smaller matters, then you will do so in larger matters.)[20] Although the form of spoken

---

[20]Luke 16:10

marriage vow words may vary, the content and words of traditional vows contain the necessary covenants for a life-long marriage. Here is a sample of these vows—

After 400 years, The Book of Common Prayer remains an official prayer book of the Church of England and the Anglican Communion. This is a Christian Wedding ceremony.

THE MARRIAGE

The Man, facing the woman and taking her right hand in his, says

In the Name of God, I, M., take you, N., to be my wife, to have and to hold from this day forward, for better for worse, for richer for poorer, in sickness and in health, to love and to cherish, until we are parted by death. This is my solemn vow.

Then shall they loose their hands; and the Woman, still facing the man, takes his right hand in hers, and says

In the Name of God, I, N., take you, M. to be my husband, to have and to hold from this day forward, for better for worse, for richer for poorer, in sickness and in health, to love and to cherish, until we are parted by death. This is my solemn vow[21].

---

21 The Book of Common Prayer, pg. 427

VOWS DONE

Having heard each other's vows, and assuming a modestly successful first marriage days, the work of achieving oneness really begins. Though the details of vows may be largely forgotten, that they were made will not. That collection of spoken covenants (which are promises) will appear as reminders of mutual commitment especially when something arises that presents a challenge to them.

As to achieving oneness, the earliest experience is sexual. The oneness experienced here is the easiest to achieve within a marriage. Amongst its functions, it is an essay in the larger marital oneness. It should be preserved as a celebration of union. It should be a mutual event in the married life. It should be an opportunity to focus upon each other exclusive of other life matters. It should not be used as a form of manipulation to other ends. I.e. We can have sex if you .... Thus, it should stand on it's own as an important part of a healthy marriage.

The sexual life is necessarily accompanied by a more general concept of exposure. Acceptance of each other's nakedness is a continuing act. Whatever our appearance is when young, it will be less attractive when old. If our oneness has moved beyond the essay of sex, then we will not be repulsed by aging flesh. We will learn how to embrace it; how to use it to embrace the other.

Exposure will bring us into contact with other matters. One key to oneness is what we do with the other's exposed weaknesses. We must learn to accept the other weaknesses to be one. If my response to your weakness is a habitual criticism, then I will be forcing you to build a wall between us. You will need that wall to fend off words that hurt. Instead of allowing you to expose a weakness, I will be forcing you to hide it, to protect it from view. Over time, that wall between us becomes a barrier to communications, and a barrier to intimacy. It is a failure to accept the other. It makes it more difficult to reveal ourselves to the other. We must certainly have kept hidden many details about our lives that are not conveyed before marriage. Putting up a wall to shield each other from items revealed makes it more difficult to feel safe exposing what was hidden. Oneness will improve as we both permit the presence of weakness in the other and unite to protect that weakness from outside attack. In that pattern of life, the wall between us is dismantled.

Exposure must also be accompanied by forgiveness. As we fail each other both directly and indirectly,(a father failing his child will indirectly fail the child's mother.), we need forgiveness. Much of this forgiveness will be unspoken as we develop a healthy pattern of not forcing each failure to receive an accusation, followed by confession, followed by forgiveness. Rather, one will observe a failure of the other, and simply forgive without words. How does this help? We are not God. We are not the judge of the other. A delicate balance is maintained by our allowing God to continue to manage our partner, and by refusing to usurp His role in that management. True forgiveness requires knowing how to not take offence at the sins of the other.

Exposure becomes a catalyst for secrets to emerge. Some secrets may never be mentioned as a healthy marriage will reduce the relevance of the past. Other experiences of ours before marriage will become necessary to address. It is quite common that victims of abuse begin to reveal that abuse years after being married. This wall of self-protection extends into more than one area of life. At some point, it becomes visible to each. And then, being visible, the desire to be healed of such a past, and to move into a greater intimacy will force such a past to be addressed.

Thus, the half of each that was hidden before marriage will be exposed in marriage to the other. How that exposure is responded to will either advance of hinder oneness between the two.

Early in the marriage, as each partner seeks to please the other, words of acceptance and assurance show approval and love. Each partner enters marriage with a previously built wall. This was constructed primarily in the then child learning from his/her parent(s). So, each partner enters a marriage with their own wall to manage.

KEYS TO BUILDING ONENESS

Marriage fails of its promises in part by having no direction afterward. It too quickly degenerates into hanging on to or acquiring common interests. The common interests demand time. The more common interests we acquire, the more our lives are supposed to have in common. We should be getting along fine. Unfortunately, too many discover that holding common interests is insufficient. Common interests are an extension of who we are. When we identify too strongly with the activity, it actually becomes a distraction. Hence, common interests are not the essence of marriage. They are an extension of ourselves.

A marriage occurs when a man leaves his family, (mentally, emotionally, and physically) and unites with his wife to become one. Thus, a new family is formed. Two further notes on this—The man and woman each leave their families differently. The spoken vows of marriage reinforce this leaving, and cleaving instead to each other. The second note--This leaving will be tested by the family members of each. This testing is somewhat natural where the skills of each are developing, especially those of a relatively unskilled partner. There will be conversations about some matter, whose subject is really the adequacy of one's spouse. Here, the response should reinforce the status of the partner as someone who has really left home. Where a partner fails to indicate this severing, much conflict can occur for years over the failure of the partner to leave his house, and cleave to his spouse.

Nevertheless, continuing to develop as one requires that each partner returns to the model of God's declaration of "becoming one." A marriage shall advance with our two becoming more one, and less two.

Another practice to adopt in becoming one is to value those moments of becoming one. Such moments carry the characteristic of strengthening the marriage bond. Meaning, there are many shared events that do not carry this characteristic.

With God's model in mind, and a few oneness experiences in memory, we can begin a habit of making decisions using a criteria of one decision result being that we will become more one. What role does each play in family decisions? Are their strengths and weaknesses considered? Making an undiscussed decision that will hurt the other is not cured by a later attempt to smooth over the resultant problems. Better to plan ahead or wait.

Remember that God is intending something other than what exists already. He is intending to make two into one. He seeks to fashion a Trinitarian Life, expressed in Trinitarian marriages, where oneness occurs.

The Trinitarian Marriage

A Trinitarian marriage is defined as a relationship including God as the third, and thus a relationship capable of expressions not centered upon procreation.

Marriage by Evolution

It is a conclusion of evolution that sex is for procreation, the survival of the fittest. No matter how complex or entertaining the sexual act might seem it is no more than a procreative ritual inspired by DNA. Words describing marriage as other than procreation stimulate the senses, etc. In the end, their only product is species perpetuation. What we own, fight over, etc. is all niche development within which species perpetuation occurs. What I might write under a category of an evolution based marriage would necessarily either develop my niche or perpetuate my offspring. Hardly a recipe for oneness.

Oneness permits a Trinitarian model to be expressed. Each partner differs from the other. Yet, within their union, they retain their particular natures. The language of Trinitarian thought about God uses the word consubstantiation. The God-head persons of the Trinity continue to exist without consubstantiation. This means that the Father does not absorb or somehow eliminate the Son. Both continue along with the Holy Spirit to inhabit their positions. They are three; they are one. So, in a marriage between a man and woman, successful oneness still finds the woman being herself, and the man himself.

Neither is diminished or absorbed. One is not consubstantiated to the other. In fact, a marriage conducted with one partner becoming so thoroughly dominate of the other is not regarded as healthy by outsiders. Rather, the loss of independence is noted, and may find itself the subject of pejorative gossip. "Why does she/he put up with that?" The partners have essentially consubstantiated. This type of unity is not modeled after the oneness of God's persons. Further, within a oneness marriage, the roles of each are not of less value than the other. If I hang pictures, and my wife controls their location, neither of us have taken a role of less value in this united task.

Oneness does require considerable unity. Thus unity occurs in the midst of each partner living out individual thoughts and pursuits.

Our married couple develops their own love content. What may look like nothing to an outsider may be but one method of love's expressions between these two. Without having read them, I have heard of discussions of "love languages". As a couple develops their love content, such expressions may indeed be classifiable as a form of love language. It takes time for these expressions to become stable. Initially, and even later, there will be numerous opportunities to choose a new way to express affection for the other. The challenge eventually becomes one of retaining meaning within a familiar set of expressions. Each will choose to give that expression meaning, one as giver and the other as recipient. These are all love's choices. Over time, and as our couple ages, these love choices will become loves necessities. There were always things I did, that she did not. Now, I do them, not just of habit, but because they need to be done and she will never do them again even if she had to. They have become part of the fuel of our union, of our oneness. Never my favorite task, I have always hung pictures even with pretended objection. Now, I would be deeply offended if she asked a stranger to take that task away from me. I do not love that task; I do love pleasing her.

A vital aspect of oneness is finding regular agreement on decisions. Early in the marriage, decision patterns are developing with less initial certainty. If a couple learns how to decide together, then some later decisions will find one partner acting on behalf of the other. This confidence in agreement takes time to grow. Many couples substitute acrimonious debate for agreement. Their lives are lived in acquiescence or opposition. Some couples make a pattern of independent acts. I remember as a child watching the Lucy show. In my memory, many episodes had to do with Lucy making some odd decision on her own, and then spending the rest of the show seeking to fool Ricky who would eventually discover the charade, and forgive Lucy. Without these deceptions, there would be no show. And so, in a marriage, much drama can be avoided, and unity achieved with a little discussion ahead of time.

Even more foundational to the oneness relationship are shared purposes. Here is where the benefits of both being Christian are most found. Having given their individual lives, and then their marriage to God, they are both seeking His will, His purposes. They each should be finding a confidence that God will direct their partner. Hence, their purposes can be unified, even when not mutually settled upon.

DANGERS

There are paths towards oneness; there are paths away from it. The paths away from oneness are hereby called "aloneness acts". Rather than two becoming one, I am doing something that preserves or advances me as a single person, living alone. An example mentioned already has been the failure to leave home so as to unite with one's spouse. Conduct that is dangerous to oneness is where one or both spouses makes a habit of having a "night out" with friends. Friendships, and comradery are good for one's existence. But, the kind of nights out where I am purposely getting away from my spouse is unhealthy for a marriage. Where I find it necessary to visit the local watering hole on the way home from work or where my nights out with my friends also become days outings away from home, then other marital duties will begin to break down. Our communications will break down into bare necessity words. Our sex lives might become even more self-focused or diminish altogether. Some of our "friends" might be bad influences, with their own collection of failed or failing marriages. They will help increase the distance between me and my spouse. Lastly, and this one can be quite common, work can destroy our oneness. As my mind never leaves the workplace, I have little room for home and family in my thoughts and actions. All of my priorities are linked to the job. There is no room for a marital discussion of them; I am too busy. Thus, I walk away from our unity towards an alone existence.

Living as one will occur in increments. As we avoid destroying our oneness, we must choose conduct to add to our oneness. We will accumulate such experiences to form oneness habits, oneness memories.

Oneness events will have one or more of the following qualities. They will seem timeless, modeling the qualities of an infinite love that we touched in courtship, pledged in marrying, They will manifest in the same way when apart. They will have a fleeting quality being something we cannot own or display on demand. There will be feedback upon our understanding of God. On occasion, we might experience love in such a way that we come to understand a little of why mortal bodies cannot come face to face with God without change. Meaning there is a very practical reason that human flesh cannot see God; it would cease to exist. Thus, we then understand a little of why we will have to be changed; mortal flesh cannot endure the unshielded love of God. Only a changed, and perfected flesh can live in heaven, in God's presence. We also then understand a little of why marriage does not endure beyond death. The intensity, and degree of God's unshielded love renders all other loves inadequate, and indeed unnecessary.

LEAVING COURTSHIP BEHIND

After marriage, the firsts diminish in number, not importance. They might now become favorites. More likely, new favorites will appear or a continuing pattern of favorites will be lived. We may both enjoy mountain vistas. Old and new vistas will be mutually enjoyed. The courtship patterns are whittled down, and transferred into marital patterns. Marital romance should replace courtship romance. The jargon of romance will become a "romantic expectation", renewable on cue by one or the other. A married couple experiencing oneness will be happy that marital oneness has replaced courtship oneness. They won't be looking backwards, mistakenly longing for courtship fantasies.

ONENESS ACCOMPLISHED

So, we have built, and continued to build a oneness marital structure. In this, we will find our twoness restructured not destroyed. As we invest in each other's talents, we will learn that one benefit of forming each other is an expansion of us. As one is set aside, the result must, and will contribute to the growth of us. We discover how self-denial is a bridge to the formation of me and you. In that pattern, we affirm us, and strengthen our oneness. If we have the privilege of more than one career, we invest together in them. My wife knows more about taxes than I ever expected she would glean from my confidential silences.

We have lived out our promised unconditional love; each of us is an active participant in us. We have moved from the struggles of negotiating oneness to the joys of living it. We have moved from the hopeful vows of love to the comfort of knowing we are loved and valued. We have moved from the experiences of youthful love to a rather mysterious mature love.

And, finally, and beyond what can be written, we are further prepared through the perfections of the images of spousal love to come face to face with the heavenly oneness embrace of Jesus Christ.

WHEN I MISSED YOU

I missed you when I left
for I knew you were not coming

I missed you as I drove up
and saw the cabin empty

And when I saw the flowers
rhododendron beauty and laurel too
I nearly cried for you to be
at my side

At the mountain top too
I missed you. (though I
don't think you would have
walked there anyway.)

I missed you passing
familiar haunts of childhood
camping

And every fire I lit
left my body warm
but my heart cold without
you to warm it

All things which were of
beauty and curious to me
had me turning to say
"Beth! Look!" but you
weren't there.

So keep your heart next
to mine in the morning hours
And go to the mountains
with me.

By: Paul Munden

Note-A poem written while away for a week
examining timber in the mountains in 1985.
Further note- We did vacation in those same
mountains that summer.

The flowers I give to thee
are arranged so carefully
a purple one here, a yellow one there
for your love's a bouquet to me.

Your warmth like the gentle spring sun
which bids the crocus forth
your eyes like the skies I love
clear and bright and blue

you've been arrayed with baby's breath
three separate and precious bouquets
you guard them as the ivy
and teach them Godly ways

Your love has the scent of roses
your petals cover our bower
a kaleidoscope of colors
a fragrance for every hour

At your heart is the lily of Easter
from this flower all love springs forth
we woke on that morning and walk to the day
where the darkness will never come

Introduce me to your mother
so I may tell of my delight
how God gave you to me
my companion always to be
My love, may I kiss you goodnight?

By: Paul N. Munden, 1995

BIBLIOGRAPHY

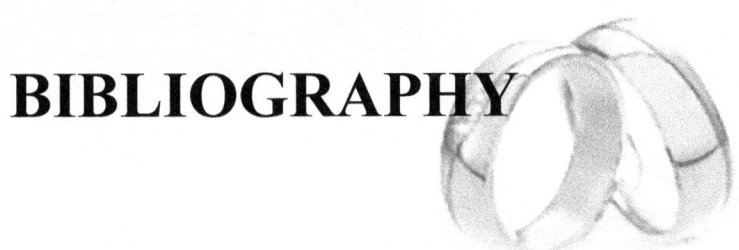

Committee on Christian Education, Inc. *Trinity Hymnal*.
   Philadelphia: Orthodox Presbyterian Church,
   1961.
The Lockman Foundation. *The Holy Bible*. La Habra, CA:
   Foundation Publications, Inc., 1995.
Websters. *Websters Dictionary.* n.d.
Church Publishing, Incorporated, The Book of Common Prayer,
   New York, 2016
Baker Books, Christian Theology 2nd Edition, Millard J. Erickson,
   July, 2004

APPENDICES

APPENDIX A

HERE'S LOOKING AT YOU KID!

An honest search of the human soul by the one possessing it produces a mixed reaction. There are parts to love and parts to hate. One question usually focuses on the parts hated. It can be worded in several ways but it amounts to this – "Why am I like this?" or "Why did I do that?"

Sometimes you leave this question unanswered; further thought is required and there isn't time. Sometimes, you answer, "I am who I am and as good as anybody" and adjust yourself to living with yourself. Sometimes, you believe people who say "everything is alright", though you still don't feel like everything is alright. And, sometimes, you stop asking the question. It is no longer your problem what you do in life. It is the problem of other people.

In the world around you, there are examples of professions who must deal with the question, "Why am I like this?"

Corporate managers hire consultants to train young and old executives to have productive, positive, outlooks. These managers recognize the relationship of self-image or self-love to production and they take steps to help their employees work through the despair that results from the self-examination which leaves the question "Why am I like this?" unanswered.

God created man to live in a peaceful relationship with God, other men, nature and himself. Harmony, not discord, was the blueprint. Mankind's decision to reject God's command resulted in a breakdown of all these relationships.

God need not define sin, issue laws, or write personal letters for you to understand what sin is. If you cannot be satisfied with everything you are and do, why do you find it so impossible to accept that God is not satisfied with everything you are and do? After all, He certainly has more at stake than you. You are concerned with yourself. He is concerned with the whole world. Your love is focuses on your own desires. He needs nothing from men and women so His love by definition must be purely voluntary. He owes us nothing. Yet, He created us, loves us, and has made inroads into humanity to resolve your inner conflicts.

My observations at the age of 16 identified humanity as the big problem in this world. Nature, although vicious and giving no mercy to the weak, functioned in an efficient cycle. Only man destroyed natures cycle and himself on a large scale. This presented a dilemma I could not resolve or excuse. I could not reason why man was so destructively different; why he did not fit in. Nor could I reason how I as a product of humanity's destructive history could avoid the same mistakes.

A couple of years later, (unplanned by me understand), I returned to my Creator and asked Him to resolve my own conflicting parts and prevent me from following the same self-destructive, hopeless course of the rest of humanity.

Thus, a process was begun in me which still continues. I will occasionally ask, "Why am I like this?" for I still see things I dislike. But, now I have assurance and evidence that God has, is, and will change what neither He nor I like about me. And better than that, He has given me evidence of positive, permanent, rearrangement of me into someone both He and I will be completely satisfied with some day.

"For God so loved the world that He gave His only begotten Son, that whosoever believeth in Him should not perish but have everlasting life."

Part of the "everlasting life' you can receive through following Jesus Christ is God's activity in the depths of your soul to transform you into the person He created you to be which will ultimately turn out to be someone you can completely love!

APPENDIX B

VALENTINES DAY

Valentine's Day offers the opportunity to express love simply. The marriage anniversary primarily affirms the marriage contract. I.e. I would choose to marry you today if you and I were single. I would choose to contract a marriage with you. And, the celebration of the contract should certainly be accompanied by love. Unfortunately, for many, that day becomes something slightly less than a birthday; something that is short will be over in a few hours as tomorrow is coming, etc.

Valentine's Day affirms love's jealously. Ie I desire to possess you. I choose to lavish my affections upon you. I desire for your affections to be wholly towards me.

It is in its simplest form that love is blinding. It is blind to the thoughts of the outsider. It is blinding in its intensity. It is incomprehensible. "How did those two ever get together?" Valentine's Day affirms the incomprehensibility of our choosing of each other.

So, what price love? Flowers, chocolate and candy have endured as appropriate symbols.

How to celebrate. It is more difficult to catch up when behind. If I am trying to convince my spouse that I prefer him/her, when a significant message is regularly sent to the contrary, then a Valentine's Day gift is insufficient to the task. I would better present a speech to my spouse about my failures first, than my adoration. If we regularly affirm how we prefer someone, then the symbol may be a very simple and heart felt expression. The recipient will know.

There is great pleasure in being hopelessly in love. Chains of affection over time provide a sense of security of belonging, the expectation of loving and being loved and a sense of purpose. Ie Someone needs to be loved by ME; no one else will do.

As you prepare to love each day the one you have promised to love, remember that Valentine's Day is coming.

APPENDIX C

A GUIDE TO RIGHTEOUS ACCOUNTANTS
BY: PAUL N. MUNDEN

Having worked as an accountant for over 30 years, the best and really only description of my work by others was approximately "you work with numbers". I typically missed the fear that went with those words. What I would say to those who took a greater interest was that accounting is really a system of thought. The numbers and math though challenging are really fairly simple. To a math major, it would seem very simple. (I may have already lost some of you.)

Math, as described, seems incredibly boring and daunting to many, including me. And yet, we can do very little without math. Of course, the other side of the challenge finds nerds like me who get caught up with the more anal aspects of math. I.e. accounting Yes, I chase pennies in bank reconciliations. One of my earliest audit tasks was to foot (meaning add) a computer printout. I was unable to successfully do this. The more senior audit manager did this, even showing me what I missed. We both cared about this test of computer accuracy. Raise your hand if you also care deeply about such things.

Well, returning to accounting theory, let me say that no matter what role you play in an accounting process, it all starts and ends with a simple equation—"Assets=liabilities + equity". This is the answer to all questions about basic financial information. Another even more exciting accounting truth is that the debits (think left side) must equal the credits (right side). Left minus right must equal zero. Example, if you take cash from a cash box and buy pencils, the cash spent equals the value of the pencils. Pencils minus cash = zero.

A complete set of financial statements is, in many ways, an interim step when all the math is correct, and the basics of accounting measurements are finished.

As time has moved on, the world of financial reporting (what you tell other interested parties about your business) continues to reach out into the more difficult to measure non-financial world with the goal of measuring, recording and disclosing relevant but really weird stuff. I mean if the main factory just burned down maybe someone should say something about the impact upon the new year. It does not help the investor so much if I only publish information about how great the prior year was. I mean, next year cannot be that good with a burned down factory.

So the accounting professional and accounting governing boards have seriously labored over rather intangible, weighty matters to identify, measure and report. I know the cost of the factory that just burned; I don't know the cost of a new one. Nor do I know the overall cost to the business enterprise of the building loss.

The final results, in our example, of all such measurements are entries to estimate what was truly lost, and the cost to recover from this loss. An account will be created, a "loss of factory" account to hold these estimates. What is an account? In general, an account may be viewed as a bucket to hold transactions. Cash is in one bucket; pencils are in another. And, "loss of factory" is another. And, then our work only gets more complex and complicated as we look at further ramifications of this factory loss. I mean, what if someone died. Apart from the tragedy of human life loss, what do you say about a likely lawsuit, and when. Finishing even this example is a lot more work.

RIGHTEOUSNESS

But, now, I want to segue into a more important matter. The Bible, God's written word to mankind, tells us about God. It tells us about ourselves. It tells us how to bridge the differences between this living God and us. In this message, words are used that accountants understand. We are accepting these words of the Bible, including the accounting words, as we proceed. To stay with God upon death our souls must be righteous. Each of us needs an account that sums to God's righteousness.

Righteousness is a desirable quality to obtain. Having enough righteousness enables us to bridge the differences between God and us. We seldom use this word—righteousness. We do find a pejorative form in use, self-righteousness. Someone who is described as self-righteous has a quality of arrogance on display. They proudly proclaim their fundamental reality as *better than most, maybe better than all.* If directly accused of fault, they deny it. But, if asked about almost anything, they will have a *final* opinion to inject. They are dangerous to have as an enemy. They do not forget insults or losing an argument. They may find themselves with very few friends. I mean, who is worthy to be in their presence? So, on being told how to bridge the differences between them and God, they will object. If asked why, they will offer several possible answers. Some summarized examples follow.

1. There is no God; thus there are no differences.

2. There is a God; the differences are minor.

3. While some of you need a bridge to God, they do not.

4. They just won't talk about it.

Of course, there are some people who have heard of this God. They have heard of this living God who is unlike them. He is so unlike them that a special word is usually applied to Him. He is Holy. Holy is a word that places God in a category of His own. He is so different from us that we cannot describe Him fully. He has a long list of qualities that are His alone. But, the Holy quality is the one that especially places Him on one side of a chasm, and us on the other. The chasm is another way of naming the *differences between God and us*. God is Holy. Included in that Holiness quality is a necessity that all that come near to Him must also be Holy like He is Holy. For all and each of us humans on the other side of the chasm, even a small difference makes us unholy. To be unholy makes us unable to live with a Holy God. You cannot mix Holy with unholy. Rather, our unholy future is to live an eternal existence in a place where God is not present. That place is named Hell. Hell is horrible, a place of suffering. No matter how much someone might wish to debate what it means to live in Hell, the most significant quality is that God is not there. He is not there to mitigate the sufferings of Hell. I would suggest that even if you would say you prefer Hell to being near God, that you would not really enjoy this choice. You would do far better to desire the Holy, not the unholy, to learn how to bridge the chasm, and so discover how you might live with this Holy God. Please settle your differences.

ACCOUNT

As previously stated, an account is a bucket to hold transactions. Humans have their own account. This account holds their personal transactions. These include both financial and non-financial. They include what you would call good and also include evil. If the sum of the transactions in a human account finds the good to be the majority, then you might conclude that a person has achieved a measure of goodness, a measure of goodness greater than evil, a measure of righteousness. Someone might look at this mixture of good and evil in the account, and consider this righteousness a tainted one. No one is perfect.

When we consider how the Holy God across the chasm measures an account total, we find that all human accounts fail to sum to a righteousness that can cross the chasm, bridge the differences to God. Their accounts are not Holy; they are unholy. In order to settle their differences with God, they need an account that sums to perfection with no evil to taint the righteous account. No one can post an account that sums to perfection. They will always fail, or fall short in that effort. That is what it means to be what was traditionally called a sinner. A sinner is someone whose righteousness total sums to something less than the Holiness of God.

CREDITED

Gospel means good news. There are four Gospels in the Bible. Four witnesses deepen and enrich the good news label. Jesus Christ lived a Holy life. His life. He established an account with His perfect righteousness. His life and death has enabled the Father to credit our account with the righteousness of Jesus. It is an entry that supersedes previous entries, perhaps like an accounting restatement. In His death on the cross, Jesus cancelled the unholy debits and credits rather than computing and journalizing a balancing entry that would only make us even. He then replaced our previously muddied, tainted, and really incurable righteousness account with His own perfect and untainted righteousness account. Thus, we are given, by gift, a new righteousness account. We obtain the righteousness of Jesus as an asset. The asset is a full and perfect value of righteousness. With Jesus perfect righteousness, our differences with God are thus settled; we can cross the chasm to Him.

As an example of this righteousness, consider Abraham of whom it is written, "Abraham believed God, and it was credited to Him as righteousness".[22] The righteousness of God was *credited* to Abraham's account. Since our own efforts at righteousness are insufficient to bridge the chasm between us and God, we need God's righteousness, a righteousness that meets both His approval and standards. As with Abraham, we acquire the righteousness of God by disclaiming our own efforts at crediting and allowing God's effort at crediting to be accurate and reliable. With God's righteousness credited to an account, we are made perfect in His sight. Our differences with God settled; we can cross the chasm to live in His presence.

---

[22] Romans 4:3

APPENDIX D

THE INFLUENCE OF THE PRO-CHOICE POSITION UPON MARITAL ONENESS

PART I
THE PRO-CHOICE POSITION

PREMISE- assigns all rights and responsibilities in the decision of child birth to the woman. The decision to bear or kill her young is hers alone. Within marriage, the husband who accepts fully the pro-choice position held by his wife must also acknowledge his wife as standing alone in the decision to bear or kill her young. Thus, the husband and wife cannot find oneness in the decision to have children, or the pregnancy. Once a child appears, the father of the child, willingly or unwillingly, becomes a legal father with both rights and responsibilities.

Oneness is only possible after a fetus becomes a child, not before. Oneness is only available to the woman who bears her young. The woman who kills her young is alone, and remains alone. Since the bearing or killing of young is so significant to the woman, the effect of being alone in this area of life makes a woman's life impossible for a man to share and impossible for a woman to request it be shared. How can she both be alone and request oneness from her husband? Indeed, he cannot be called "father" until she consents to the existence of a child. He cannot accept the term "father" until the fetus becomes a child. The man is a nothing in relationship to the product of conception. He is a father by law at the successful birth of a child.

The adoption of either a pro-choice or pro-life position affects the range of reactions to and decisions concerning pregnancy. These positions also affect marriage. They must. Pregnancy and childbirth are life dominating events for the mother. The birth of one child changes many lives. For example, consider the many phones calls that occur as a new mother holds her child in the hospital room. She or the father or both are on the phone passing out new names. Names such as, "grandfather", "grandmother", "brother", "sister", "aunt", "uncle" are distributed. Other terms such as "cousin", "great" or "step", etc. include even more people. Having illustrated just how large and broad these events are to families, our concern here is very narrow. And, our starting point in the timeline of marriage is a couple without children, a couple not even yet married. How do these two positions affect a man and woman in love? How do these two positions affect their discussions? Does one or the other more facilitate the sharing of their lives? What measure of marital oneness are they able to later achieve?

Marital oneness might be described, in part, as the sharing of two lives. An active developing relationship naturally and continuously creates opportunities for sharing. We want to speak of ourselves; we want the other to "open up", to speak of themselves. We choose to do things together to share experiences. We share a bowling experience. We don't go dancing. We share walks beside the lake. We don't stroll along crowded streets. We attend a sports event. We avoid the wax museum. We find special places where we verbally relate our life histories. We share coffee at Starbucks, not the convenience store. We dine at restaurants where romantic corners are available. We do not take stools at the lunch counter. Even as we are enjoying fresh moments of life together, we are always talking. The less crowded venues are less distracting. There we talk with more depth. If those conversations fail to advance our knowledge of each other, if nothing personal is shared, then the relationship will likely end. There are not enough activities to experience in the present for the relationship to lead to marriage if nothing deeper is happening. Further, we test the conversations with our beloved by sharing some of them with others whose opinions we respect. Even as we suspect that love is blinding us, we will alternately revel in the joy of the blindness or seek help in seeing the matter more clearly through the eyes of a counselor. Ultimately, to commit to a lasting relationship, we must become convinced that we have, and will continue to have, enough in common, and that the differences between us are and will remain acceptable. We find out what the other does for a living, what they do for fun and how their family is structured. We learn of tastes in food, hobbies, and dislikes. We discuss the future, including children, towards learning if our individual future plans will enable us to walk together as husband and wife. We will also converse about weightier subjects that inform our decision making processes, religion and politics. Finally, when we have sufficiently shared our lives to reach a decision to marry, we will formally and publicly marry.

After we marry, we begin to share our lives as they really are. Before we marry, we share those parts of our lives we wish the other to see. No matter how successfully we conveyed ourselves to the other before marriage, there is so much to now learn of the other that it seems as though we married knowing almost nothing. The distance between an arranged marriage where the husband and wife meet each other for the first time on the wedding day is not really so great from that of the couple that dated in advance of marriage. As we now realize how little we know of each other, those subjects left "for after we are married" will surface. Those areas of life which we really are not inclined to share will be identified. Life experiences too painful to share before will now begin to emerge. The marriage vows play an extremely important role in sharing after marriage. We will be reminded by our mutual declaration to share our lives together that we must try again to do just that. (Pain, anger, and denial do not make subjects disappear.) If we are reaching a little higher, if we continue to hunger to share our lives with each other, we are still aiming for oneness. It is a healthy marriage that is managed towards developing and maintaining a pattern of sharing. The areas of life unknown to the other should decrease over time. From phone calls during the work commute to discussions while we sit together at children's soccer matches to lazy Saturday mornings where we catch up with news of last weeks events, we keep the blood flow of shared lives coursing through our marriage.

Areas of life we do not share, if significant to our marriage, are like blocked veins or arteries. Or, to use another image, they are like closed off rooms of a house. In both of these illustrations, the rest of the body and house may be reasonably healthy and active. Some couples live their entire marriages in the knowledge of and endurance of the unshared. "We don't talk about that." What is revealed after death or divorce about the unshared life is both surprising and sobering.

In our culture, the marital language concerning the subject of children has drastically changed. With the advances of medicine, infant mortality has decreased as well as the number of deaths of mothers in childbirth. Men no longer marry younger sisters to replace the wife lost in childbirth. Infant through teenage grave stones are still very painful, yet less frequent. With the introduction of contraception, abortion and artificial methods of conception, the timing and very existence of our children is more likely the subject of discussion. It is in the discussion of children that the pro-choice view influences marital oneness.

The pro-choice position must be considered against the larger backdrop of reproductive freedom. Women do not want simply the right to kill their young through abortion. They want reproductive freedom. The reasons women want reproductive freedom, and the relationship of reproductive freedom to the rights of women in general is a subject of considerable debate among women. Therefore, the following is acknowledged as a sample of reasoning rather than a definitive reasoning.

Reproductive freedom is connected with a woman's independence from her own biology. Primarily through contraception and abortion, she is freed from the bondages of ovulation, fertilization and gestation. These are not necessarily thought of as bondages in the sense of slavery and shackles, though to some they are. More often, they are bondages in that they were historically beyond her control. Strongly associated with being events beyond her control is their connection to men. Ie A man has power over her through his ability to trigger these events in her. He also stands fundamentally free from these bondages since the cost to his body is very small, whereas the cost to her body is very great. With regards to sexual pleasure, the cost to his body in relationship to his pleasure is also small, whereas her bodily cost is significant, even deadly. Reproductive freedom is thus an equalizing force. Having gained control over ovulation, fertilization and gestation, the woman is freed from these costs, these bondages. The natural consequences of sex, inherent in her biological nature, are under her control. She may pursue sexual pleasure as freely as a man. She is free to choose when and if children are a consequence of her pleasure.

To be pro-choice is to hold abortion up as both a symbol and an act. It is a symbol to affirm and live out the benefits of reproductive freedom, and an act to terminate one's own offspring. The emphasis upon the symbol facilitates the marginalization of the offspring. It becomes for "my own good" that I dehumanize and eliminate what is in me against my will. What will rule my life? Will I be free to continue my pursuits and pleasures or will this thing inside of me remind me of him and bind me to the servitude of motherhood? "Think of your own future". As long as the best decision made is viewed as that which projects my maximum, unchained, individual autonomy, then the presupposition of pregnancy as a severely limiting factor upon my maximum, unchained individual autonomy leads easily to the conclusion of an abortion as best for me.

This unchained autonomy is associated with a publicly expressed desire for the existence of universally available medical procedures. When a neighborhood abortion clinic closes, it is a potential loss of freedom depending on how far it is to drive to another clinic. When partial-birth/late term abortions are eliminated from the pool of choices, then it is a loss of freedom. I can possess all the rights to choose I wish. If facilities are not available to exercise that choice, I am effectively again in bondage. For, I must be able to actually exercise control to be effectively free.

Another absolutely essential element of reproductive freedom worth further emphasis is the vesting of the power to choose life or death for one's offspring in the woman alone. She must be able to walk into the clinic unaided, and unrestrained physically, mentally and psychologically. Thus, reproductive freedom also requires that others, especially men, more particularly the biological source of the semen have no right in a pregnancy. Ovulation, fertilization and gestation occur inside a woman's body, not the man's. She is the sole ruler of her own body. She, alone, possesses the decision making power concerning the existence of offspring.

Being the sole ruler over her choice makes it necessary to stand alone in her choice. It is, as they say, "lonely at the top". Relatives may freely tell her what to do because, they actually "know what is best" for her. Properly trained counselors will objectively tell her that it is "her decision alone". They would not dare to choose for her legally or psychologically. While it may be wise to respectfully hear out the various recommendations from the various voices around her, it is her power to decide, her choice to make. For being absolutely alone in her choice is what results from possessing true reproductive freedom. The counselor will, of course, generously support her decision. However, it remains her decision. Afterwards, it was her choice alone that was exercised, not the choice of relatives or counselors. She has exercised her choice.

To be pro-choice means to be alone. It means that the critical life decision of giving birth, of becoming a mother, cannot be truly shared with anyone. Any breech of the walls of the fortress of reproductive freedom opens herself to a loss of freedom. No man may enter, not even the one with whom she otherwise chooses to share all of her life. She is a Rapunzel in a tower of her own creation. For pleasure alone, he may climb her golden stair. For a discussion of children, and the sharing of pregnancy, he must remain outside.

Rapunzel is now alone in her tower. She has power over the offspring of the prince. He has no power to enter the tower without her permission. To gain complete rule over her pregnancy, she defined her connection to the prince as completely severed. The fact that he issued semen to contribute to the existence of the child does not change her rights. He is not a father or would be father by the contribution of semen alone. He is essentially not a father until she chooses to give him that name.

This is the picture of our pro-choice woman. She is fully committed to her beliefs without any doubts. Included in the shared values of our now married couple is her husband's commitment to accept or at least respect her pro-choice position.

Before discussing further Rapunzel's marriage, let's consider how her prince might generally respond to his pro-choice Rapunzel. If pro-choice is true for a woman, what must a man conclude concerning himself? He may accept her pro-choice position either willingly or unwillingly. He may be truly "pro-choice", and thus embrace her position with open arms. He may regard himself as "pro-choiced", begrudgingly accepting his powerlessness. He may see marriage to a pro-choice woman as making him a truly "no choice" man. Childbirth is her decision entirely. The issuance of semen, though technically a potentially procreative act, is now primarily an erotic act. He need only concern himself with the erotic. She is totally responsible for the procreative. His only responsibility is to see that she enjoys the erotic. He has no responsibility for the procreative. Should she accidentally become pregnant, he has no role in the choice of the bearing of the young or the killing of the young. He has no responsibilities in the results of her choice. He has no right to rejoice or grieve in her decision.

RAMIFICATIONS OF BEING ALONE IN CHOICE

A married couple knows when their lives are shared or hidden from each other. Some examples of sharing and hiding follow. Sex is a shared act. When sex goes into hiding, it may take the forms of adultery or pornography. Finances are shared. There may be one bank account. Hidden, excessive spending is evidence of an unshared financial life. We raise our children together. When I say of a child, "he's your problem", I am saying that we will not share the raising of this child. I have a career that provides for the family, and provides significance to my life. You may share in those career decisions, whether job changes, physical moves or advancement. When I say "it's my life", I am saying that I have no interest in your sharing this part of my life with me. A marriage where problems are significant is typically described as a list of areas where we are doing well, and areas where we are not. The areas where we are doing well are shared or at least not unshared. Areas where we are struggling are closed off to each other for discussion and change. They are hidden or unshared.

A pro-choice woman, by definition, is defined as alone in the decision to bear or kill her young. This area of marriage cannot be shared. To be pro-choice is to be alone.

Example 1. Her husband, having agreed that their lives will be lived in a pro-choice world, is content for their marriage to be childless. A two career childless marriage enables a full "sharing" of sex, finances and careers. Thus, should her heart move towards a desire to bear her young, her pro-choice (childless) minded husband may not appreciate at all her desire to interpret choice anew as the bearing of her young. He will correctly point out that her choice to bear her young will affect their shared sex, finances and careers. Ie reduced/changed sexual lives, loss in income/lifestyle, change in career for her/change in career priorities for him. Their pro-choice marriage may end over this debate between two pro-choice people about the practical marital definition of pro-choice.

A pro-choice woman, by definition, is defined as alone in the decision to bear or kill her young. This area of marriage cannot be shared. To be pro-choice is to be alone.

Example 2. She decides to have a child by her husband. In singling out her husband to be the father, and in choosing to involve her husband in discussions about the decision to bear her young, she must entirely abandon pro-choice jargon. Rapunzel is choosing a different life. She is dismantling the tower entirely. Her pro-choice husband is startled by the change. Nevertheless, he was always secretly a man who wanted a child. He loves his wife, and was willing to share all he could with her even if they could not share a discussion about children. That area of marriage was by definition of pro-choice hers alone. Now she tells family and friends "we" are expecting our first child. She wants his help. At times during the pregnancy, she needs his help. What could not be shared is shared. The realization that sharing is necessary and is actually happening is as disturbing to their pro-choice views as the events of the pregnancy. They learn daily that the pro-choice rhetoric is unworkable in marriage if they are to share pregnancy and children together. There is a struggle to this change. It is not an easy transition to a new way of thinking. They were quite unprepared for it.

THE REAL CHOICE

To be pro-choice is to be fundamentally alone in decisions concerning childbirth and pregnancy. Such a position carries over into marriage as an area of life that cannot be shared with a husband. Further, a pro-choice husband must also accept a very limited role in childbirth and pregnancy. His role as a male figure in the marriage is fundamentally limited in that his role in procreation is muted. The introduction of a wanted pregnancy into such a marriage will require a tortured restructuring of language and thought for the husband to be permitted to share this area of life with his wife. Without her approval, he would never be able to call the child "ours" without this language change. Should the effort to restructure their marriage towards some unity of thought not be made, and this area remain by definition unshared, the couple will not be fundamentally unified in the most challenging venture of marriage, the raising of children. In some measure, the child will remain more hers than his. In a world where imperfect men are prone to abdicate their responsibilities as fathers, the pro-choice position greatly reduces the personal angst of the absent father. For women who "change their mind" regarding the desirability of their two-year old, their own personal guilt in abandoning the child to the father is a return to pro-choice lifestyle whereby the child has no claim upon her life and heart.

CONCLUSION

"The hand that rocks the cradle rules the world". This old saying will likely evoke a number of negative responses. The one observation I wish to make is that it is multi-generational. If the cradle is empty, then all else that the woman values is likely to pass away with her relatively short life. That makes the very survival of a culture dependent upon the presence of children. And, that makes the choice of a woman a social, not just a personal decision. The values of those cultures that choose to place a child in the cradle are those that will survive. The pro-choice woman who chooses to kill her young is also in the process of eliminating the pro-choice position. The pro-choice woman who bears her young must step outside of the language of reproductive freedom to justify the existence of "father" and the use of such phrases as "our" child. The current construction of the pro-choice position leaves her alone in her choice, and makes this an area of life that cannot be shared with her husband. Thus, marital unity in the area of childbirth and pregnancy is impossible. Since our concern here is with marital unity, a change in thought is necessary for the sake of marital oneness.

APPENDIX E

THE INFLUENCE OF THE PRO-CHOICE POSITION UPON MARITAL ONENESS

PART II--THE PRO-LIFE POSITION

Sex is not for procreation alone. It is not for pleasure alone. It is both a pleasurable and procreative act. The emphasis of one over the other always produces an incomplete social result. It was not difficult for men and women to circumvent a social view that sex was for procreation alone. They were, after all, still enjoying sex. Nevertheless, they had usually been taught that the sexual act had a larger significance, which some were willfully ignoring in fornication. Under the pro-choice position, sex is only for pleasure. The sexual act has no larger significance. Virginity becomes an obstacle to pleasure. With a cultural emphasis upon irresistible hormones, and not denying ones urges, would be virgins have little more than delay tactics to employ in resisting sexual activity. So, a greater responsibility becomes difficult to attach to the sexual act. Nevertheless, sex should be regarded as both a pleasurable and procreative act, as designed to be located within a monogamous marriage.

Vesting the sexual act again as an equally pleasurable and procreative act assigns multi-generational significance to every aspect of sex. Semen again has social significance. Male and female virginity have value. The male and female who wish to prepare for marital unity will not waste themselves in misguided sexual activities that betray the possibility of marital unity.

Abortion on demand may remain a legal option. However, the ritualistic (procedure as ritual for the abortion zealots) killing of one's young to affirm women's reproductive freedom is one of the great evils of our time. Disconnecting the philosophies from the abortion procedure separates the ritual aspect from the act, leaving the procedure to exist more simply as the intentional killing of one's offspring. In this procedure, a child dies. The death of the child is an occasion of grief, and a welcoming event in heaven. If performed to fulfill the pleasure, desire and will of the mother, it is a terrible and unnecessary procedure. This woman is alone in her choice, and alone in her grief. She has not been freed from the "bondages" of biology. Rather, biology now reigns supreme. She has now chosen a barren flesh that will be accompanied by a barren mind and soul. How will she ever find anything significant in the sexual act beyond physical sensations? No assurance of being cared for or cherished beyond her responses to stimuli. No ability to require her lover/husband to see anything significant in her giving of herself to him. No ability to require him to own up to the significance of his own semen.

THE PRO-LIFE OPTION

Most medical advances in contraception are viewed favorably by pro-life women. Abortion on demand is not a favorable option. A pro-life position fundamentally embraces all pregnancies as gifts of the God who gives the miracle of life. Having embraced the concept that a new life will reside in her, she is free to admit her husband into planning for that life. She is free to speak of herself as carrying "our" child. She is never alone in her choice being in a position to share the joys and struggles with others including her husband.

www.ingramcontent.com/pod-product-compliance
Lightning Source LLC
Chambersburg PA
CBHW051230120626
46547CB00013B/1586